# First World War
and Army of Occupation
# War Diary
France, Belgium and Germany

7 INDIAN (MEERUT) DIVISION
Divisional Troops
4 Cavalry
9 August 1914 - 30 November 1915

WO95/3936/1

The Naval & Military Press Ltd
www.nmarchive.com
Published in association with The National Archives

Published by

## The Naval & Military Press Ltd

Unit 10 Ridgewood Industrial Park,

Uckfield, East Sussex,

TN22 5QE England

Tel: +44 (0) 1825 749494

www.naval-military-press.com

www.nmarchive.com

*This diary has been reprinted in facsimile from the original. Any imperfections are inevitably reproduced and the quality may fall short of modern type and cartographic standards.*

© **Crown Copyright**
**Images reproduced by permission of The National Archives, London, England, 2015.**

# Contents

| Document type | Place/Title | Date From | Date To |
|---|---|---|---|
| Heading | WO95/3936/1 4 Cavalry | | |
| Heading | 7 Meerut Division 4th Cavalry 1914 Aug-1915 Nov | | |
| Heading | War Diary of 4th Cavalry From 9-8-14 To 30-11-14 Volume I | | |
| Heading | War Diary of 4th Cavalry From 1-12-14 To 31-12-14 Volume I | | |
| War Diary | Bareilly | 09/08/1914 | 03/09/1914 |
| War Diary | Bombay | 06/09/1914 | 20/09/1914 |
| War Diary | Marseilles | 12/10/1914 | 16/10/1914 |
| War Diary | Orleans | 18/10/1914 | 27/10/1914 |
| War Diary | Merville | 29/10/1914 | 29/10/1914 |
| War Diary | Locon | 31/10/1914 | 03/11/1914 |
| War Diary | Gorre | 03/11/1914 | 09/11/1914 |
| War Diary | Locon | 12/11/1914 | 30/11/1914 |
| War Diary | Croix Marmeuse | 01/12/1914 | 18/12/1914 |
| War Diary | Le Touret | 18/12/1914 | 18/12/1914 |
| War Diary | Croix Marmeuse | 19/12/1914 | 19/12/1914 |
| War Diary | Le Touret | 20/12/1914 | 21/12/1914 |
| War Diary | Croix Marmeuse | 21/12/1914 | 22/12/1914 |
| War Diary | Le Touret | 23/12/1914 | 23/12/1914 |
| War Diary | Croix Marmeuse | 24/12/1914 | 24/12/1914 |
| War Diary | Robecq | 25/12/1914 | 25/12/1914 |
| War Diary | La Miquellerie | 26/12/1914 | 31/12/1914 |
| Heading | War Diary of 4th Cavalry From 1st January 1915 To 22nd January 1915 | | |
| War Diary | La Miquellerie | 01/01/1915 | 25/01/1915 |
| War Diary | Amettes | 25/01/1915 | 31/01/1915 |
| Heading | War Diary of 4th Cavalry From 2nd February 1915 To 28th February 1915 | | |
| War Diary | Amettes | 01/02/1915 | 02/02/1915 |
| War Diary | Les Lobes | 03/02/1915 | 12/02/1915 |
| War Diary | Le Hamet Billet | 13/02/1915 | 23/02/1915 |
| War Diary | Les Lobes | 24/02/1915 | 26/02/1915 |
| War Diary | Le Cornet Malo | 27/02/1915 | 28/02/1915 |
| Heading | War Diary 4th Cavalry From 1st March 1915 To 31st March 1915 | | |
| War Diary | Le Cornet Malo | 01/03/1915 | 01/03/1915 |
| War Diary | Quentin | 01/03/1915 | 01/03/1915 |
| War Diary | Hingette | 02/03/1915 | 06/03/1915 |
| War Diary | Richebourg St Vaast | 10/03/1915 | 11/03/1915 |
| War Diary | Hingette | 13/03/1915 | 14/03/1915 |
| War Diary | Lestrem | 24/03/1915 | 31/03/1915 |
| Heading | War Diary of 4th Cavalry From 1st April 1915 To 30th April 1915 | | |
| War Diary | Carvin | 01/04/1915 | 01/04/1915 |
| War Diary | Lestrem | 10/04/1915 | 12/04/1915 |
| War Diary | Carvin | 23/04/1915 | 27/04/1915 |
| War Diary | Lestrem | 25/04/1915 | 30/04/1915 |
| Heading | War Diary of 4th Cavalry From 1st May 1915 To 31st May 1915 | | |

| | | | |
|---|---|---|---|
| War Diary | Lestrem | 01/05/1915 | 06/05/1915 |
| War Diary | Rue De Vaches | 06/05/1915 | 08/05/1915 |
| War Diary | Croix Marmeuse | 09/05/1915 | 10/05/1915 |
| War Diary | Les Lobes | 11/05/1915 | 15/05/1915 |
| War Diary | La Couture | 16/05/1915 | 16/05/1915 |
| War Diary | Les Lobes | 16/05/1915 | 31/05/1915 |
| Heading | War Diary of 4th Cavalry From 1st June 1915 To 30th June 1915 | | |
| War Diary | Les Lobes | 01/06/1915 | 05/06/1915 |
| War Diary | Calonne | 06/06/1915 | 29/06/1915 |
| Heading | War Diary of 4th Cavalry From 1st July 1915 To 31st July 1915 | | |
| War Diary | Calonne | 01/07/1915 | 13/07/1915 |
| War Diary | Thiennes | 21/07/1915 | 21/07/1915 |
| War Diary | Estaires | 29/07/1915 | 31/07/1915 |
| Heading | War Diary of 4th Cavalry From 1st August 1915 To 31st August 1915 | | |
| War Diary | Estaires | 01/08/1915 | 03/08/1915 |
| War Diary | Neuf Berquin | 04/08/1915 | 27/08/1915 |
| War Diary | Les Puresbecques | 27/08/1915 | 31/08/1915 |
| Heading | War Diary of 4th Cavalry From 1st September 1915 To 30th September 1915 | | |
| War Diary | Les Puresbecques | 01/09/1915 | 29/09/1915 |
| War Diary | La Bassee Road | 25/09/1915 | 25/09/1915 |
| Heading | War Diary of 4th Cavalry From 1st October 1915 To 31st October 1915 | | |
| War Diary | Les Puresbecques | 01/10/1915 | 03/10/1915 |
| War Diary | Cornet Malo | 04/10/1915 | 19/10/1915 |
| War Diary | Pont D'Hinges | 04/10/1915 | 19/10/1915 |
| War Diary | Calonne | 20/10/1915 | 31/10/1915 |
| War Diary | Les Puresbecques | 01/10/1915 | 03/10/1915 |
| War Diary | Cornet Malo | 04/10/1915 | 19/10/1915 |
| War Diary | Pont D'Hinges | 04/10/1915 | 19/10/1915 |
| War Diary | Calonne | 20/10/1915 | 03/11/1915 |
| War Diary | Campagne | 04/11/1915 | 07/11/1915 |
| War Diary | Thiennes | 07/11/1915 | 18/11/1915 |
| War Diary | Tolel Kebin | 19/11/1915 | 30/11/1915 |

WO 95/293 6/1

4 Cavalry

7 Meerut Division

4th Cavalry

1914 AUG — 1915 NOV

To MESPOT 6 CAV BDE

D.I./Kearne

War Diary
4th L. Cavalry.
From 9-8-14
to 30-11-14.
Pp 1 to 3
Volume I

War Diary
of
4th Cavalry
From 1-12-14
To 31-12-14
Volume I
Pp 4 to 6

121/1046

Army Form C. 2118.

# WAR DIARY

or

## INTELLIGENCE SUMMARY.

(Erase heading not required.)

Instructions regarding War Diaries and Intelligence Summaries are contained in F. S. Regs., Part II, and the Staff Manual respectively. Title pages will be prepared in manuscript.

[Stamp: ADJUTANT GENERAL IN INDIA — 10. DEC 1914 — BASE OFFICE]

| Hour, Date, Place. | Summary of Events and Information. | Remarks and references to Appendices. |
|---|---|---|
| BAREILLY 6 pm 9. VIII. 14 | Mobilization Ordered | During the period Nov 3rd to 15th the majority of the men were absent from their homes practically the whole time. Owing to this and the bad weather the recruit's training and equipment has been constantly interrupted. Owing to the non arrival of stores needed for, especially oil and dubbin, arms and equipment were almost impossible to keep clean and in several cases the cordite in the |
| 4 pm 21. VIII. 14 | Mobilization Completed | |
| 3 pm 3. IX. 14 | Entrained for Bombay | |
| BOMBAY 8 am 6. IX. 14 | Arrived BOMBAY encamped COLABA | |
| " 15 IX 14 | Embarked on S.S. NAMORA and EURYALUS | |
| 9 " " | Sailed | |
| 12 Noon 20. IX. 14 | | |
| MARSEILLES 11 am 12. X. 14 | Arrived MARSEILLES encamped LA VALENTINE | |
| 12 noon 16. X. 14 | Left MARSEILLES | |
| ORLEANS 5 pm 18. X. 14 | Arrived ORLEANS | |
| 12 noon 27. X. 14 | Left ORLEANS | |
| MERVILLE 10 am 29. X. 14 | Arrived MERVILLE. Detached one Sqn. as escort G.O.C. 2 A.C. | |
| LOCON 2 pm 31. X. 14 | Concentrated 3 Sqns at LOCON | |
| 3 pm 1. XI. 14 | 150 of all ranks employed in digging reserve trenches at CROIX BARBEE | |
| 4 pm " | 1 Sqt. Ret: the one Sqn attached 2nd Ind Inf Bde at GOREE | |
| 12 noon 2. XI. 14 | " " " " LE TOURET | |
| 11 am 3. XI. 14 | 105 men employed digging trenches at CROIX BARBEE remainder of Regt. moved to LOCON | |
| GOREE 3.30 pm " | Regt less one Sqn. concentrated at GOREE furnishing 130 rifles in support of 2nd Ind. Inf. Bde | |
| " 6.30 pm 4. XI. 14 | Regt less 1 Sqn furnished 150 rifles for Reg. U. trenches trenches 3 miles | |
| from Nov 5th to NOV 11th | | Considering that the |

Army Form C. 2118

# WAR DIARY
## or
## INTELLIGENCE SUMMARY.
*(Erase heading not required.)*

Instructions regarding War Diaries and Intelligence Summaries are contained in F. S. Regs., Part II, and the Staff Manual respectively. Title pages will be prepared in manuscript.

| Hour, Date, Place. | Summary of Events and Information. | Remarks and references to Appendices. |
|---|---|---|
| Nov 4 | CAPT HOTHAM JEMADAR HARNAM SINGH was wounded (British and one Indian officers) [Rank] and ill one invalided. The Somras were left at BETHUNE - being posted in the open - one have died - owing to whole of the time the weather has been very wet and mostly with intermittent rain. The Regiment was supplied with Bayonets. | Regiment was of [danger] for trenches and after had baggage digging support as convenient from trenches. It is possibly had few our casualties has been as the various parties were in a temporary [base] |
| LOCON 1 pm 12.xi.14 | Regiment has 5g'd returned (-Rifles) at LOCON | |
| 11 am 13.xi.14 | C Sq'n relieved 'D' Sq'n escort to G.O.C. 7A.C. at VIEGES. | |
| 4 pm 13.xi.14 | Received a digging party of 200 men under 4 British officers at CROIX BARBÉE, these men on duty till 4:30 am 14. Not one man was killed. | |
| 1 pm 15.xi.14 | 50 British roorkis to 21st Ind. Inf. Bde, which were posted in trenches. | |
| | Machine Gun Section under Capt Thomson reinforced 2/39th GURWAL RIFLES at ANDE IRELON. | |
| 2.3 pm 5.xi.14 | 100 of all ranks under Co. Bahadur to LE TOURET and formed. | |
| | SUPPORT PETRIE | |
| 6 and 7th Nov | Ex Rifles at LOCON | |
| 2.30 pm 18.xi.14 | Demanded digging party of 200 men at LE TOURET. Despatched them but to bright ambushed at 9 am. | |
| 3 pm 19.xi.14 | Bamboo for 3 hours returned at 3.30 p.m. | |
| | One Indian ran slightly and one man severely wounded. | |

# WAR DIARY
## or
## INTELLIGENCE SUMMARY.
*(Erase heading not required.)*

Army Form C. 2118

3

| Hour, Date, Place. | Summary of Events and Information. | Remarks and references to Appendices. |
|---|---|---|
| LOCON 3 p.m. 20.xi.14 | Furnished digging party. Dorsrmen at GOREE who relieved 21.xi.14 one man slightly wounded. | During the period 15-22" Nov. the men suffered |
| 3 p.m. 21.xi.14 | As above 15 o'men who returned midnight | much from cattle and chafed feet owing to the fact |
| 11.30 a.m. 22.xi.14 | Regiment moved to Billets at FOSSE and LESTREM | that they had to march to 2 a.m. 23.xi.14 |
| 2 a.m. 23.xi.14 | H.Q. action reported Ref. | the work in trenches in both |
| 2.30 p.m. 24.xi.14 | A. & B." proceeded to HINGES and trouble party of 210 and moved to LACROIX MAMEUSE. | was unacceptable for the purpose as weather Trenches in both |
| | B. & "C." in front of German Trenches from LOCON | has been very front. and the |
| 25.xi.14 | Billets at CROIX MAMEUSE and Foret | ordnance line it had been |
| 7 a.m. 26.xi.14 | Furnished digging party of 30 men near GOREE Party returned 5 p.m. | all it ought but the redout and waiting for replacement |
| 6.15 — 27.xi.14 | In Billets. | |
| 28.xi.14 | Furnished party of 130 men for clearing Aerodrome near CRATERS | |
| | DE WERPPE in Billets. | |
| 29.xi.14 | Furnished party of 130 men for digging trenches near GOREE | |
| 7 a.m. 30.xi.14 | Party returned 5 p.m. | |

1.XII.XIV

A.J.M. Mainwaring Lt. Col.
Comdg. 4th Cav.

# WAR DIARY
## or
## INTELLIGENCE SUMMARY.

Army Form C. 2118

(Erase heading not required.)

Instructions regarding War Diaries and Intelligence Summaries are contained in F.S. Regs., Part II, and the Staff Manual respectively. Title pages will be prepared in manuscript.

| Hour, Date, Place. | Summary of Events and Information. | Remarks and references to Appendices |
|---|---|---|
| 8.30 am 1.12.14 Croix Marmeuse | 3 British Officers, 8 Indian Officers and 100 men were sent to LOCON for inspection by H.M. King George. | |
| 3.30 pm 2.12.14 " | Capt. Howson and 16 men with 2 machine guns detailed for duty in the trenches with the 19th Infantry Brigade near Richebourg. Rest of the Regiment less one Squadron at HINGES in billets. | |
| 3.12.14 " | In billets | |
| 4.12.14 " | Marched to LOCON and went in to billets there. A Squadron reported from Corps Headquarters. | |
| 11 am | 2 B.O.'s, 2 I.O.'s and 120 men were sent to FESTUBERT to dig trenches. Party returned at 11 P.M. 1 man wounded. | |
| 3 hr | | |
| 3.30 hr 5.12.14 | Furnishes digging party of 100 men at FESTUBERT. Party returned midnight. 4 men slightly wounded, 1 man killed | |
| 3.30 hr 6.12.14 | ditto as above 150 men 1 man killed | |
| 3.30 hr 7.12.14 8.12.14 | Capt. Robert BRADLEY relieved Capt. HOWSON in charge of the machine guns in the trenches In billets LOCON | |
| 9.12.14 10.12.14 11.12.14 12.12.14 | Moved to billets at CROIX MARMEUSE and FOSSE 1 man killed in machine gun section | Transferred 4 horses to Remount Depôt. Retain or write for further orders. |
| 13.12.14 | In billets. Capt HOWSON relieved Capt BRADLEY in trenches | |

Gulab Singh & Sons, Calcutta—No. 22 Army C.—5-8-14—1,07,000.

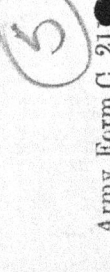

Army Form C. 2118

# WAR DIARY
## or
## INTELLIGENCE SUMMARY.

*(Erase heading not required.)*

Instructions regarding War Diaries and Intelligence Summaries are contained in F. S. Regs., Part II, and the Staff Manual respectively. Title pages will be prepared in manuscript.

| Hour, Date, Place. | | Summary of Events and Information. | Remarks and references to Appendices |
|---|---|---|---|
| | 14.12.14 CROIX MARMEUSE | In billets | During the month of December the weather has generally been cold, raw and wet. But notwithstanding this both the men and the horses have kept wonderfully well. |
| | 15.12.14 " | do | |
| 9.15am | 16.12.14 " | Furnished digging party 253 all ranks near LA COUTURE | |
| " | 17.12.14 " | Ditto | |
| | | Capt. BENTON relieved Capt. HOWSON with machine guns in trenches attached GARHWAL BDE. | |
| 9.15am | 18.12.14 " | Furnished digging party as above | |
| 2.30pm | " LE TOURET | Moved Regiment to LE TOURET as divisional reserve | |
| | 19.12.14 CROIX MARMEUSE | Returned from LE TOURET. 1 Horse died | |
| 2.30pm | | | |
| 1pm | 20.12.14 LE TOURET | Moved Regiment to LE TOURET as divisional reserve | |
| 10am | 21.12.14 " | Occupied and improved reserve trenches E of LE TOURET. 1 Horse destroyed for Tetanus | |
| 5pm | " CROIX MARMEUSE | Returned to billets CROIX MARMEUSE | |
| | | Capt. PEARCE relieved Capt. BENTON with machine guns section in the trenches | |
| 12.30pm | 22.12.14 " | Proceeded to LE TOURET and occupied reserve trenches E of LE TOURET | |
| 9am | 23.12.14 LE TOURET | Returned to Billets at CROIX MARMEUSE. 1 Horse shot & Horses sent to mobile Vet Section | |
| 11.30am | 24.12.14 CROIX MARMEUSE | Regiment marched to ROBECQ and billeted for the night | |

Army Form C. 2118

# WAR DIARY
## or
## INTELLIGENCE SUMMARY.

(Erase heading not required.)

Instructions regarding War Diaries and Intelligence Summaries are contained in F. S. Regs., Part II, and the Staff Manual respectively. Title pages will be prepared in manuscript.

| Hour, Date, Place. | Summary of Events and Information. | Remarks and references to Appendices |
|---|---|---|
| 11 am 25/12/14 ROBECQ | Regiment marched to Billets in LA MIQUELLERIE In Billets at Date | |
| 26/12/14 LA MIQUELLERIE | " | |
| 27/12/14 " | Captain PEARCE and Machine gun section relieved | |
| 7 pm " " | In Billets | |
| 28/12/14 " | " | |
| 29/12/14 " | " | |
| 30/12/14 " | " | |
| 31/12/14 " | Between November 2nd and 27th December the Machine Gun Section has been in the trenches for 41 days under Capt HOTHAM 4 days, Capt HOWSON 20 days, Capt BRADLEY 6 days, Capt BENTON 4 days, and Capt PEARCE 7 days. Lately they have been attached to the GARHWAL Bde. Major General KEARY VC, CB Commanding the Brigade has written to me his thanks and appreciation of the good work done by the Section whilst attached to the Highlanders tho't Col Comby 4th Cavalry. | |

# WAR DIARY

of

4. Cavalry.

From 1st January 1915 to 22nd January 1915.

1st patrol

**Army Form C. 2118.**

# WAR DIARY
## or
## INTELLIGENCE SUMMARY

*(Erase heading not required.)*

Instructions regarding War Diaries and Intelligence Summaries are contained in F.S. Regs., Part II, and the Staff Manual respectively. Title pages will be prepared in manuscript.

ADJUTANT GENERAL INDIA — 3. FEB. 1915

No. 3 BASE OFFICE
A. G's Office at ...
I. E. Force
Passed to ... S. Sect<sup>n</sup>
on 3-2-15

| Hour, Date, Place. | Summary of Events and Information. | Remarks and references to Appendices |
|---|---|---|
| January 1st 1915 to January 25th 1915 LA MIQUELLERIE | In Billets. Refitting. Ordinary daily parades both mounted and dismounted. Training of British Cavalry guides and Patrols. Training of extra men in machine gun. 16 Indian Officers, 40 NCOs and British Officers not otherwise employed, attended a class of Instruction in Field Engineering under the 107th Pioneers daily. | 2nd January Jemadar SULIMAN KHAN joined from Base. 22nd January 18 Sowars joined from Base. Casualties Personnel 25th Jan. 1 man died. Between 4th Jan and 21st Jan 15 sick evacuated. Between 2nd Jan and 24 Jan 4 men reported from Hospital. Horses Jan 3rd 8 Remounts received. During January 2 Horses destroyed 3 Horses died 4 Horses sent to Mobile Vet. Section. During January the whole of the Regiment was inoculated. |
| 10.30 AM Jan 25th – Jan 31 AMETTES | Marched to new billets at AMETTES. Ordinary daily parades | |
| January 22nd | Captain G HOWSON, 2 Guides and 17 Rank & File joined GARHWAL Brigade at RICHEBOURG. | |

H/Stenfelt/Lt Col
Comdg 4th Cavalry

Serial No 69

WAR DIARY

4th Cavalry

From 2nd February 1915 to 28th February 1915

Original

Army Form C. 2118.

# WAR DIARY
or
## INTELLIGENCE SUMMARY.

(Erase heading not required.)

Instructions regarding War Diaries and Intelligence Summaries are contained in F. S. Regs., Part II, and the Staff Manual respectively. Title pages will be prepared in manuscript.

| Hour, Date, Place. | Summary of Events and Information. | Remarks and references to Appendices |
|---|---|---|
| AMETTES 12.15 " 2.2.15 | In Billets. Ordinary daily work | Casualties. Personnel between 1st & 28th Feb. |
| 9.30 a.m. " 2.2.15 | Marched to new billet at LES LOBES and TORPE BILLOT | 31 Sick Evacuated |
| 3.2.15 to 12.2.15 LES LOBES | Ordinary Daily Work Cutting Brushwood | 7 Men reported from HQrs Reinforcements |
| 3.2.15 | Machine Gun Section under Captain Howson | 25th Feb 1 2nd Officer and 47 R & F joined |
| 8.30 am 12.2.15 LE HAMET BILLET | Returned to new billets at LE HAMET BILLET | Horses 1st to 28th Feb Received 15 |
| 23.2.15 to | In Billets. Ordinary daily work. Captain Howson with Machine Gun Section attached to DEHRA DUN Bgde on 23.2.15 | Remounts destroyed 5 Horses cast 9 to Mobile Vet Sec 6 |
| 23.2.15 to 24.2.15 LES LOBES | Marched to LES LOBES | |
| 10.30 a.m 26.2.15 | | |
| 1 pm 27.2.15 LE CORNET MALO | Marched to Billets at LE CORNET MALO | |
| 28.2.15 | | |

A.H. Kennafun[?] Maj[?] T.Col
Comdg 4 Cav

# WAR DIARY

## 4th Dn. Cavalry.

From 1st March 1915 to 31st March 1915

# WAR DIARY
## or
## INTELLIGENCE SUMMARY.

*(Erase heading not required.)*

Army Form C. 2118.

Instructions regarding War Diaries and Intelligence Summaries are contained in F. S. Regs., Part II, and the Staff Manual respectively. Title pages will be prepared in manuscript.

| Hour, Date, Place. | Summary of Events and Information. | Remarks and references to Appendices |
|---|---|---|
| March 1st – 9th LECORNET MALO QUENTIN HINGETTE | In Billets. Ordinary work | Casualties Personnel 1 B.O. to Hospital 6 men wounded 16 men sick evacuated Rejoined from Hospital 5 Reinforcements 24 R&F 2 B.O.S. Horses 7 draps 14 Inf Horses R.d. 6 Horses destroyed 4 " 6 Petite Velha |
| March 2nd | Capt BRADLEY relieved Capt HOWSON with Machine Gun Section in trenches | |
| 6th | Capt HOWSON relieved Capt BRADLEY | |
| March 10th RICHEBOURG S.t VAAST | Arrived 4.30 a.m as Reserve to Meerut Division to operations around NEUVE CHAPELLE | |
| 11th–11pm | Moved to Trenches S.W of NEUVE CHAPELLE 2 British Guides & 6 men wounded 5 Officers in M.G. Section | |
| 10am 13th HINGETTE | Returned to Billets at 7 PM | |
| 9am 14th & 23rd " | Machine Gun Section arrived from Trenches | |
| 9am 24th to 30th LESTREM | Lt Col Macquaid Assumed daily work. Army Corps Commander inspected Regt 23rd Marched to new Billets N.W. of LESTREM | |
| 1pm 31st " | Capt BRADLEY transferred to R.F.C. 28th Marched to new Billets at CARVIN | |

# WAR DIARY

## OF
## 4th Cavalry

From 1st April 1915 To 30th April 1915

**Army Form C. 2118.**

# WAR DIARY
*or*
## INTELLIGENCE SUMMARY.
*(Erase heading not required.)*

Instructions regarding War Diaries and Intelligence Summaries are contained in F. S. Regs., Part II, and the Staff Manual respectively. Title pages will be prepared in manuscript.

*Stamp: ADJUTANT GENERAL INDIA, BASE OFFICE, 3 MAY 1915*

| Hour, Date, Place. | Summary of Events and Information. | Remarks and references to Appendices |
|---|---|---|
| 1.4.15 CARVIN | In billets. Usual daily work | Casualties. Personnel. Between 1st & 30th April |
| 11am 10.4.15 LESTREM | Marched to LESTREM | Men admitted to hospital 7 |
| 12.4.15 | Motion gun section under Captain LAWSON was attached to BAREILLY Bde. in the trenches near CHAPIGNY. Reinforcements to |  |
|  | Rest of MG Section gave usual parades daily | 2 British officers 10 R.E.F. Horses Casualties |
| 1pm 23.4.15 CARVIN | Marched to CARVIN | 5 Horses missing to battle of Chokes |
| 3pm 27.4.15 | Usual gun section rehearsal |  |
| 10.5am 26.4.15 LESTREM | Marched to LESTREM | 3 " to battle of Chokes Personnel |
| 30.4.15 | Usual gun section parades daily | 2 W.C.O. Gunners ASC Other 2 Sepoys Lascars Enrolling Numbers 8365 Wagoners Mules & ASC attached to Regt |

*Signature: A/Stanfield? Lt Col*
*Commanding 4th ... Cavalry*

Serial No 67.

121/5799

# WAR DIARY
## OF
### 4th Cavalry

From 1st May 1915 To 31st May 1915

Army Form C. 2118.

# WAR DIARY
## or
## INTELLIGENCE SUMMARY.

(Erase heading not required.)   4TH CAVALRY

Instructions regarding War Diaries and Intelligence Summaries are contained in F. S. Regs., Part II, and the Staff Manual respectively. Title pages will be prepared in manuscript.

| Hour, Date, Place. | Summary of Events and Information. | Remarks and references to Appendices |
|---|---|---|
| May 1st to 6th LESTREM | In Billets Usual daily work. | Casualties Personnel 1st to 31st May |
| 11am May 6th RUE DE VACHES | Marched to new billets RUE DE VACHES | 22 R & F evacuated Sick |
| May 8th " | Usual daily work | B.o.S. Tr. dets. 1 man died of wounds |
| 6am May 9th CROIX MARMEUSE | Marched to CROIX MARMEUSE. In state of instant readiness | 1 B.O. rejoined from Hospital Reinforcements R & F = 11 |
| May 10th " | " " | 1 N.C.O. A.S.C. transferred England |
| 4pm May 11th LES LOBES | Marched to LES LOBES In state of instant readiness | Horses Casualties 6 destroyed |
| 3am May 15th " | Ditto | 10 to Base Vet Section |
| May 16th LA COUTURE | Remolayerem LA COUTURE | Remounts 15 riding |
| 6pm May 16th LES LOBES | In billets LES LOBES | 8 draughts |
| May 29th " | Ditto | |
| May 29th " | " | |
| May 31 " | In billets LES LOBES | |

HG Stanefurth Lt Col
Com dg 4th Cav
31/5/1915

Serial No 64.

# WAR DIARY
## OF
### 4th Cavalry.

From 1st June 1915. To 30th June 1915.

Army Form C. 2118

# WAR DIARY
## or
## INTELLIGENCE SUMMARY.

(Erase heading not required.)

4TH CAVALRY

Instructions regarding War Diaries and Intelligence Summaries are contained in F. S. Regs., Part II, and the Staff Manual respectively. Title pages will be prepared in manuscript.

| Hour, Date, Place. | Summary of Events and Information. | Remarks and references to Appendices |
|---|---|---|
| June 1st to 5th LES LOBES | In billets. Usual daily work. | Casualties Personnel June 1st to 30th |
| 12 noon June 6th CALONNE to June 30th " | Marched to new billets near CALONNE Usual daily work | 12 R&F India evacuated sick 1 British Officer " 1 O.R. British " Rejoined |
| 4.30 p.m June 18th | Lt General Sir J Willcocks inspected the Regiment mounted on the Canal bank N of LESTREM | 2 R&F Ind from Hospital 1 from Reinforcements Horses |
| 12 noon June 24th | 1 NCO and 10 R and F with one Machine gun was placed at the disposal of G.O.C. 13 MAE 1624 1324. | 4 Horses evacuated to Mobile Veterinary Section 2 returned to permanent Depot Sick of D.D.R. Received " Remounts |

H G Stansforth Lt Col
Comdg 4th Cavalry

Serial No 67.

121/6502.

WAR DIARY

4th Cavalry

From 1st July 1915 to 31st July 1915

Army Form C. 2118.

# WAR DIARY
## or
## INTELLIGENCE SUMMARY.  4th Cavalry

*(Erase heading not required.)*

Instructions regarding War Diaries and Intelligence Summaries are contained in F. S. Regs., Part II, and the Staff Manual respectively. Title pages will be prepared in manuscript.

| Hour, Date, Place. | Summary of Events and Information. | Remarks and references to Appendices |
|---|---|---|
| July 1st to July 21st CALONNE | In Billets. Usual daily work | Casualties Personnel July 1 - 31 |
| July 13th 10 p.m. | Machine Gun Section rejoined Headquarters | 5 R&F Rank increased |
| July 16th 9/30 p.m. | Capt FARRAN and LT HEIGERS, 4 IOs & 105 OR. were attached to BAREILLY B.G. on the transfer and were posted in the last two cases than V! | 1 OR Furlot 1 followers Rejoined |
| July 19th 10 p.m. | Above detachment rejoined Headquarters. Man Rupally Horses | 3 R&F from Hospital |
| July 21 THIENNES 2.30 p.m. | Headquarters proceeded to Billets near THIENNES | 2 horses to Vet for destroyed 3 " " |
| July 29 ESTAIRES 9 a.m. to July 31 do. | marched to Billets at ESTAIRES | |

Hy Stanfords? Lt Col.
Com'dg 4th Cavalry.

Serial No 67.

12/6948

# WAR DIARY
## OF THE
### 4th Cavalry

FROM 1st August 1915 TO 31st August 1915

Army Form C. 2118.

# WAR DIARY
## or
## INTELLIGENCE SUMMARY. 4TH Cavalry

(Erase heading not required.)

Instructions regarding War Diaries and Intelligence Summaries are contained in F. S. Regs., Part II, and the Staff Manual respectively. Title pages will be prepared in manuscript.

| Hour, Date, Place. | Summary of Events and Information. | Remarks and references to Appendices |
|---|---|---|
| 1915 August 1st–3rd Estaires | In Billets. Usual daily work | Casualties Personnel August 1st – 31st 3 R&F Evacuated Rejoined 1 O R Bridish 3 O R J British Honours to Mob Vet Indian Permanent Retained 12 Reinforcements 1 B O 1 I O 90 O RS Indian 1 O R British |
| 9.45 pm August 4th NEUF BERQUIN till | Marched to NEUF BERQUIN. Usual daily work. British Officers and detachments from each Squadron instructed in fire and bomb throwing under the Divisional Bomb Officer & Indian Officers |  |
| August 27th do | do |  |
| 3.46 pm Aug 27th LES PUSESBESQUES to Aug 31st | Marched to LES PUSESBESQUES Divisional 27 ORs |  |
| do | do Detachments |  |
| 5 pm August 1st till August 15th | One Machine gun with detachment of 6 in trenches with Bareilly Brigade |  |
| 8.30 pm August 16th 27th | Fond Garrison Dreadnought Redoubt 1 BO 2 IOs 31 ORS |  |
| 6.30 pm August 16th 20th | ditto GRANT Redoubt 1 BO / IO 4s ORS |  |
| 6.30 pm August 16th 20th | ditto North Tillery " 1 BO 1 IO 40 ORS South Tillery " 1 BO 1 IO 30 ORS " 1 BO 1 IO 40 GRS |  |
| 3.30 pm Aug 27th to 31st | ditto Church |  |

H S Crawford / Col
Comdg 4th Cavalry

Serial No 67.

121/7286

# WAR DIARY
## OF
### 9th Cavalry

From 1st September 1915 To 30th September 1915

Army Form C. 2118.

# WAR DIARY
## or
## INTELLIGENCE SUMMARY.  4TH CAVALRY

(Erase heading not required.)

Instructions regarding War Diaries and Intelligence Summaries are contained in F. S. Regs., Part II, and the Staff Manual respectively. Title pages will be prepared in manuscript.

| Hour, Date, Place. | Summary of Events and Information. | Remarks and references to Appendices |
|---|---|---|
| 1915 Sept 1–30th LES PURESBECQUES | In Billets  Usual daily work. | Casualties  Personnel  Sept 1st – 30th |
|  | Detachments | 2 IOs evacuated to Hospital |
| Sept 1 12 noon | Church Post  1 BO. 1 IO  40 ORs relieved & joined Headquarters | 3 O.Rs " |
| Sept 1 – Sept 9 | North Tilleroy  1 BO. 1 IO  40 ORs garrisoned Post | 1 OR Killed |
|  | South Tilleroy  1 BG  1 IO  30   " | Wounded  3 |
| Sept 9th | LAFONE  1 BO. 1 IO  40 ORs garrisoned Post | Horses |
|  | COLVIN   ditto | 16 Horses to Mob Vet Sec |
| Sept 16th | LAFONE & COLVIN garrisons relieved and rejoined Headquarters | Reinforcements |
| Sept 8th | Marched from Pecten 2 BOs; 1 IO  32 ORs placed under orders of Gen. | 13 O.Rs |
|  | Staff Present Division for work in front line | 1 follower |
| Sept 24th | Marched from Pecten rejoined Head quarters | 10 Horses |
| Sept 25th – LA BASSEE Road  5am | Regiment moved to Rendezvous on Estaires – LA BASSEE Road |  |
|  | Major Grimshaw & Capt Wilson with 3 IOs and 112 ORs employed |  |
|  | in evacuation of prisoners on BACQUEROT Road |  |
|  | A Squadron employed in escort of prisoners from Pont du HEM |  |
|  | 6 BOUT DEVILLE |  |
| 7 30 Pm  Sept 25th | Marched back to LES PURES BECQUES |  |

HS Manifort? Lt Col
Comdg 4th Cav.

Serial No. 67.

# Confidential

121/7601

## War Diary

of

4th Cavalry.

FROM 1st October 1915. TO 31st October 1915.

Original

C²/179.

Army Form C. 2118.

# WAR DIARY
or
# INTELLIGENCE SUMMARY.  4TH CAVALRY

(Erase heading not required.)

Instructions regarding War Diaries and Intelligence Summaries are contained in F. S. Regs., Part II, and the Staff Manual respectively. Title pages will be prepared in manuscript.

| Hour, Date, Place. | Summary of Events and Information. | Remarks and references to Appendices |
|---|---|---|
| Oct 1st - 3rd LES PURES BECQUES 9 am 4th CARNET MALO and 10th PONT D'HINGES | In billets. Usual daily work. Marched to billets at CARNET MALO and Pont d'Hinges. | Casualties Personnel Killed in action 1 I.O. 10 R Ind Wounded 10 R Ind |
| 19th | Usual daily work | Accidental death 1 I.O. |
| 2:45 pm 20th CALOUINE to 31st | Marched to billets at CALOUINE. | 1 O.R. Ind 40 R Ind |
| October 5th to 5th | Usual daily work. Captain HUDSON 21 RIDGERS and Machine Gun Section placed under orders of MEERUT Division | Horses 10 to Mob. Vet Sec 1 Destroyed Reinforcements 2 O.R. Ind Returned from I.F. H 30 R Ind |
| October 6th to | Furnished garrison of 120, 120 of 4 hours for front line system posts LOMBARTIE and ORCHARD. | |
| October 10th | | |

H.J. Scrinfourth /Col
Comdg 4th Cav

Meerut DIV Troops

Army Form C. 2118.

# WAR DIARY
## or
## INTELLIGENCE SUMMARY. 4TH CAVALRY

(Erase heading not required.)

Instructions regarding War Diaries and Intelligence Summaries are contained in F. S. Regs., Part II, and the Staff Manual respectively. Title pages will be prepared in manuscript.

| Hour, Date, Place. | Summary of Events and Information. | Remarks and references to Appendices |
|---|---|---|
| Oct 1st – 3rd LES PRESBEQUES 10 am 4th CORNET MALO and 19th to PONT D'HINGES | In billets. Usual daily work. Marched to billets at Cornet Malo and Pont d'Hinges. Usual daily work. | Casualties Personnel Killed in action 1 I.O. 10 R Ind Wounded 10 R Ind Evacuated Sick 1 I.O. 2 O.R. Bat 40 R Ind |
| 2.45 pm 20th CALONNE to 31st | Marched to billets at CALONNE. Usual daily work. Captain HOWSON Lt HEILGERS and machine gun section placed under orders of Meerut Division. | Horses Mob. Vet Sec 10 to 1 destroyed. Reinforcements 2 OR Ind returned from I.F.A 30 R Ind |
| October 6th to 8th | | |
| October 6th to October 15th | Furnished garrison of 1 I.D.O. 1 I.O. & 400 R's for fort SPOILBANK and ORCHARD. | |

IX

ASStanfastt/Col
Comdg 4th Cav

Meerut Div Troops

Army Form C. 2118.

# WAR DIARY
## or
## INTELLIGENCE SUMMARY. 4TH Cavalry

(Erase heading not required.)

Instructions regarding War Diaries and Intelligence Summaries are contained in F. S. Rgs., Part II, and the Staff Manual respectively. Title pages will be prepared in manuscript.

| Hour, Date, Place. | Summary of Events and Information. | Remarks and references to Appendices |
|---|---|---|
| November/October 1st–3rd Caloone | In Billets. Usual daily work. Arrived Campagne 15/30 pm | Personnel 1 man rejoined from I.F.A. Horses Remounts 15 Fm B foeden 1 M. Sec. 6 Distagen 1 Died 4 |
| 4th Campagne to 7th | | |
| 2/30pm 7th Thiennes | Marched to Billets Thiennes | |
| 9am 8th | March to Bergette and entrained | |
| night 10/11th | Detrained Marseilles | |
| 7am 11th | Embarked SS Janus & Saturn Chorn. | |
| 11am 17th | Arrived Alexandria | |
| kept 3km 18th | Disembarked and entrained for Tel el Kebir | |
| to 22nd 19th Tel el Kebir | Encamped at Tel el Kebir | |
| 23rd to SS Janus 30th | Entrained for Suez and embarked on SS Janus for Basra | |

H. Stanforth Lt Col
Com dg 4th Cav

(2)

www.ingramcontent.com/pod-product-compliance
Lightning Source LLC
Chambersburg PA
CBHW081502160426
43193CB00014B/2563